THANKS TO JEAN-DANIEL

FIRST PUBLISHED IN THE UNITED STATES OF AMERICA IN 2004 BY UNIVERSE PUBLISHING
A DIVISION OF RIZZOLI INTERNATIONAL PUBLICATIONS, INC.
300 PARK AVENUE SOUTH
NEW YORK, NY 10010
WWW.RIZZOLIUSA.COM

2004 2005 2006 2007/10 9 8 7 6 5 4 3 2 1

TRANSLATION BY ALEXANDRA BONFANTE-WARREN
PRINTED IN BELGIUM
ISBN: 0-7893-1210-7
LIBRARY OF CONGRESS CONTROL NUMBER: 2004104612

CLAUDINE DESMARTEAU

I'M NOT JEALOUS!

how to beat the mean greens

UNIVERSE

MY NAME'S THOMAS.
I'M PRETTY GREAT,
BUT IT BOTHERS ME
A LITTLE THAT I'M JEALOUS
OF MY PAL PAUL
BECAUSE HIS RED TRUCK
IS BIGGER THAN MINE

Lemme have your truck a coupla minutes, so I can compare it to mine
IN YOUR DREAMS

PAUL, HE'S JEALOUS
OF LUCAS, WHO HAS
A YELLOW MOTORCYCLE
THAT'S EVEN BIGGER
THAN PAUL'S RED TRUCK

LUCAS is FIERCELY JEALOUS of PETER, WHO HAS A COMPLETE SET of SUPER-RARE YU-GI-OH! CARDS

PETER IS JEALOUS
OF ROMAN BECAUSE
ROMAN WON'T SHUT UP
ABOUT HIS VACATION
IN ASPEN AND HOW HE WON
A SECOND-PLACE STAR
IN THE BUNNY SLOPE RACE

ROMAN IS TOTALLY JEALOUS OF ANTHONY BECAUSE ANTHONY TALKED TO LEAH FOR AT LEAST 5 MINUTES, AND THE CREEP WOULDN'T EVEN TELL HIM WHAT THEY GOSSIPED ABOUT

ANTHONY IS JEALOUS
OF COLIN, WHO HAS
A HUGE BEDROOM
ALL TO HIMSELF.
MEANWHILE, POOR ANTHONY
HAS TO SHARE HIS
TEENY TINY ROOM WITH
HIS STINKY BUTT KID BROTHER

COLIN IS JEALOUS
OF CELINE BECAUSE
CELINE'S FATHER
BOUGHT HER THE LATEST
VIDEO GAME, TOO DEADLY,
WHILE COLIN'S MUST BE
6 MONTHS OLD
AT LEAST AND
ALL FALLING APART

CELINE IS JEALOUS OF
LOOK-AT-ME LISA,
WHO NEVER GOES ANYWHERE
WITHOUT HER WEENSY
CELL PHONE THAT MAKES
THAT DUMB LITTLE MUSIC
EVERY TIME SHE GETS
SOME LAME MESSAGE FROM
HER STUPID FRIEND JENNIFER

Let me see your cute little phone
NO WAY, I'VE GOT A TOP SECRET TEXT MESSAGE
CU LATR!
DEEDLY DOODLY BEEP

LISA IS JEALOUS OF MELISSA, WHO'S SHOWING OFF HER AUTOGRAPHED POSTER OF BILLY CHEESEFACE TO THE WHOLE SCHOOL, AND WHO'S JUST SO SURE SHE'LL GET CAST FOR STAR HUNT

MELISSA IS JEALOUS OF MARGOT, WHO IS VERY PROUD OF HER PRETTY MOM, WHO ALWAYS DRESSES SO COOL, WHEREAS MELISSA'S MOM IS, FRANKLY, FAT AND HAS BAD HAIR

MARGOT'S MOTHER
IS JEALOUS OF BOB'S MOTHER
BECAUSE BOB'S MOTHER
CAN LIE AROUND, RUNNING ERRANDS
AND DOING HOUSEWORK
ON HER OWN SWEET TIME,
WHILE MARGOT'S MOTHER
WORKS 35 HOURS A DAY
FOR A RELENTLESS BOSS WITH
ABSOLUTELY TOXIC BREATH

BOB'S MOTHER IS JEALOUS
OF TOM'S MOTHER BECAUSE
WHEN BOB'S MOTHER'S HUSBAND
LOOKS AT TOM'S MOTHER,
HIS EYES GET ALL GLASSY,
LIKE A FRIED HERRING'S,
BUT MAINLY IT'S BECAUSE
TOM'S MOTHER IS A LOT
YOUNGER THAN BOB'S MOTHER

TOM'S MOTHER, OR RATHER
HER HUSBAND, IS JEALOUS
OF JORDAN'S FATHER BECAUSE
JORDAN'S FATHER MAKES
SOMETHING LIKE THREE TIMES
AS MUCH MONEY
DOING HALF AS MUCH WORK,
AND BECAUSE IT'S OUTRAGEOUS
THAT ANYONE GETS PAID
THAT MUCH TO DO SO LITTLE

JORDAN'S FATHER IS JEALOUS OF GERARD, JORDAN'S FATHER'S EX-WIFE'S NEW HUSBAND, BECAUSE HIS ROTTEN KIDS CALL THEIR NEW DAD "PAPA GERARD", PROBABLY JUST TO GET ON HIS (JORDAN'S FATHER'S) NERVES

THE EX-WIFE OF JORDAN'S
FATHER'S HUSBAND – NO WAIT –
OF JORDAN'S MOTHER'S HUSBAND,
IS JEALOUS OF GASPARD,
HER NEW HUSBAND'S SON, BECAUSE
HE GETS A LOT MORE PRESENTS
THAN SHE DOES: FOR CHRISTMAS,
HIS BIRTHDAY, AND EVEN WHEN THERE'S
NO REAL REASON IN THE WORLD
TO GIVE THIS LITTLE LOSER ANYTHING
PLEASE NOTE: GROWN-UPS CAN ALSO BE JEALOUS OF KIDS

GASPARD IS JEALOUS OF ZORAN,
HIS FATHER'S NEW WIFE'S SON,
FOR A LOT OF GOOD REASONS:
ZORAN IS MUCH BIGGER,
MUCH STRONGER,
HAS A LOT MORE FRIENDS,
AND IS ALLOWED TO WATCH
"TEMPTATION ISLAND" ON TV,
AND GASPARD ISN'T

ZORAN IS JEALOUS
OF HIS WHOLE CLASS,
BECAUSE HIS LAST NAME
IS "ZUBROWSKA",
SO HE'S ALWAYS
THE LAST ONE
IN ROLL CALL
(IT'S NEVER FUN BEING LAST)

ALL THE KIDS IN ZORAN ZUBROWSKA'S CLASS ARE JEALOUS OF ABDELKADER ABDALLAH, WHO IS VERY PROUD OF THE FACT THAT HE HANGS WITH ZINEDINE ZIDANE. APPARENTLY ABDELKADER EVEN BEATS HIM AT SOCCER ACTUALLY, WE'RE NOT SURE THIS PART IS TRUE

If you're such good friends, why can't we meet him?
I'M PROTECTING HIM FROM ANNOYING FANS

ABDELKADER ABDALLAH
IS JEALOUS OF
ZINEDINE ZIDANE'S SON,
BECAUSE ZINEDINE ZIDANE
SHOOK HANDS
WITH THE PRESIDENT
(AMONG OTHER STAR CELEBS)
THIS, I THINK, IS REALLY TRUE

AND THE PRESIDENT
IS JEALOUS OF ME,
THOMAS, BECAUSE
I'VE GOT A GREAT
TOY TRUCK, AND
HE DOESN'T.
WOW, LIFE JUST
ISN'T FAIR, IS IT?

POOR PREZ,
I FEEL SORRY
FOR HIM.
I DO.
REALLY,
I DO
Lucky
little
so-and-so